Fireflies

Sonnets to light the dark

Donal O'Farrell

The Swirling Leaf Press

www.swirlingleafpress.com
info@swirlingleafpress.com

Book design by Mash Chudasama
www.mash-design.com

First edition printed in 2023
ISBN: 978-1-915766-05-2

Fireflies

Sonnets to light the dark

Donal O'Farrell

The Swirling Leaf Press

For: Tomás, Ben, Róisín, Luke & Fionn

Life is like stepping into a boat
that is about to sail out to sea and sink.

—Shunryu Suzuki

We give up the past to the objector, and yet we hope.

—Ralph Waldo Emerson, *The Oversoul*

There's a thread you follow. It goes among
things that change. But it doesn't change....
You never let go of the thread.

—William Stafford, *The Way It Is*

How easily it glows,
how easily it goes out—
the firefly.

—Chine-jo

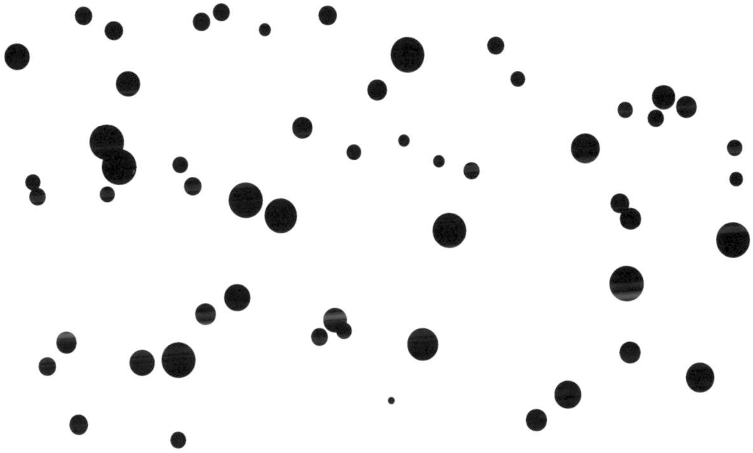

Contents

1.
Flame –
30th September 2005

(for Anne)

There comes a point in every journey
When the path appears to fail
And we can no longer travel
As simply me and me.
But if we take the fire
Of the dark night's brightest star
And know that that is who we are
In our mutual desire,
Then a living that is dying
Deeper than the grave,
A way of being
More than how to behave,
Will keep love's first true spark
Still the flame that lights the dark.

2.
Psalm

I do not know what road this is,
Darkness is my lamp,
Confusion my only compass,
Still, onwards I limp.
I do not know what name you
speak,
Silence is my prayer.
Though hope is lost, yet hope's
ethic
Holds past and future
In this moment's frail embrace.
Seduced by despair,
Drowning in this pool of darkness;
Is anyone there?—
The psalm of sacred loneliness.
Only the sightless know your face.

3.
Soar
(what the eagle said)

You must become a bridge
Across the chasm of your love.
Move closer to the edge,
Learn to sense the view from above.
Begin with simple steps—
A kind word, some small disclosure.
Get out of your shared depths,
Subject the heart to exposure.

You know the kingdom lies within
So strike the rock but once
And when the river flows you swim
Without a backward glance
Each to the other's distant shore.
Lost in currents new you may soar.

4.
Parable

(imo Jonathon Corrie, died 1st Dec 2014)

Perhaps I'll invent
A religion of my own,
Live outside the tent
To celebrate the unknown.
With these empty hands
I'll offer at the table;
Through these pathless lands
I'll walk a new parable.

Lost in the desert—
The wilderness inside,
I walk the abundant earth
With nothing to show or hide.
Living beneath the stars,
Dying at someone's door.

5.
Beatitudes

Jesus was a nomad
On the road to Calvary
With no place to lay his head
On that lonesome journey.
Jesus was a vagabond,
Hookers and *junkies* his kind.
He wandered through the holy land
When it was just Palestine.
He chased the bankers from the
temple,
Was scorned by the pharisees.
His message was simple:
Lovc, love your enemies!
Not doctrinal exactitudes;
Just parables and beatitudes.

6.
Sailing to Nineveh

It is not I who steers this boat,
Not my hand upon the tiller.
It's you who keeps me afloat,
You command the weather.
Each night as I sleep
I fall to your embrace,
You hold me in the deep,
Deliver me when I surface
On to morning's shore.
It's you who guides my steps
Through whatever door
Has unfolded while I slept
And I emerge out of the ferment
Once again your reluctant servant.

7.
The Banquet

(with thanks to Robert Frost & Derek Walcott)

Two roads diverged in the woods
And truth got left behind,
Back there at the crossroads
While I'm out wandering blind.
He's sitting by the side of the road
Waiting for Jesus to come along
To somehow lighten his heavy load,
Call him, heal him, hear his song.
Me, I'm just trying to be good,
Chasing that lonely illusion
Of the shouldn't and the should,
Still seeking that final solution.
Perhaps someday when we are old
We'll meet and feast upon our soul.

8.
Boniface
(learning to fall)

(with thanks to Mary Lavin)

When I was lost in the storm
You came to rescue me,
With your guileless charm
You set me free.
While I languished in the city
You were Kavanagh's angel
Ministering to me
With wise counsel.
You taught me our true calling,
How love works like gravity
And we are forever falling
Into the arms of Mystery.
Let go, there's nothing to be gained,
You said, and nothing to defend.

9.
Abyss

You are my oldest friend,
My earliest memory,
Without beginning or end,
You are boundless mystery.
You came trailing fear
Into my soul-dark night
But you held my stare
Until the darkness burned bright.
You gave the gift of silence
And blessed stillness—
Your peace like a violence,
Your healing an illness
That breached all my defences,
Surpassing all my senses.

10.
Rivers

(with thanks to Beatrice Bruteau)

Two lovers embracing,
An encounter of souls;
Two mirrors facing,
A universe unfolds.
Two or more gathered—
Is anyone there?
Galaxies of dark matter,
And stars strewn everywhere.

We burn to plumb the darkness,
Each soul is but a flame,
A shadowy caress;
Whispers of the nameless name—
Spondic rivers flowing plenty,
Ever emptying, never empty.

11.
Super Moon, May 2020

How many deaths did they say?
How many more infected?
How many more days to stay
Inside these walls we've erected?
It's true, the sky seems bluer,
This super moon shines so bright;
And this silence rings truer
Than all the words they write.
So as I take my nightly ramble
Through neighbourhoods in
lockdown,
While politicians dissemble
And joust with media clowns,
I watch it all from above;
Through it all I walk with love.

12.
Emerge

$E = mc^2$
Energy escaping matter—
Who we really are
Is neither here nor there.
But still we harbour lust
For what seems solid,
Reducing all to rust,
And matter made squalid.
And so we are engaged
Transforming the marvellous,
Relentlessly unassuaged—
We are *homo covetous…*
But, for now, butterflies still emerge
To dance in sunlight, to surge.

13.
Return

$E = mc^2$
And energy is love
And love is awareness—
So the universe evolves.
Each soul in its entanglement
Throbs with that sacred rhythm,
So let not our estrangement
Silence the cosmic hymn
That sings in our veins.
For we are held in common
With mountains and plains,
With river, sea and salmon.
So, may all our lost journeying
Become one with that great
returning.

14.
Choose

(imo George Floyd)

$E = mc^2$
So, let imagination
Rather than delusion
Be our guiding star.
You said our problems can't be
solved
With the same blighted thinking
From which they have evolved
But we go on drinking
From that poisoned well;
We cling to flag and nation,
Preaching a gospel
Of fear and separation.
What if we choose to see things
whole?
To realise – we are one soul.

15.
Gethsemane

It's hard to focus,
A struggle to stay awake.
All promise seems bogus,
A dawn that never breaks.
And now this meeting point
Where all roads converge
Is but the breaking point
From whence they diverge.
Ahead lies that hill
Where reason departs,
Where suffering distils
In the crucible of the heart
Into a poisoned cup.
Choose life, you say. Drink up!

16.
Crucifreed

Do I grasp your hand
Or do you take mine?
When I surrender—
Not my will but thine—
It seems our relationship
(Our two souls intertwined)
Is a Möbius strip
That forever unwinds;
That truth and mystery
Are two sides of a coin
Spinning to infinity,
Collapsing in time.
One nails me to a tree,
The other sets us free.

17.
Bodhisattvas

(for Thay)

Those bodhisattvas in Vietnam
Who made their offering of fire,
Were they embodying the flame
That we all already are?
Was that the ultimate tonglen,
An act of transfiguration?
Or was it hope befriending
Desperation?

Awareness is our true element.
Like fish below and birds above
We soar on wings of sapience
Into a reciprocal sky of love.
And still the world burns from wilful
    blindness
But we have recourse to loving-
    kindness.

18.
Fire Ants

(for Greta Thunberg & David Attenborough)

In a world of paradox,
Where exception proves the rule,
A wayward child invokes
The wisdom of the fool.
Where tree-dwellers unmoor
To leave their drowning culture,
Whose essence is fire,
And become river.
Would that we might learn
A lesson so absurd,
That the call to turn,
Long heedless and unheard,
Would become our living prayer,
Our hope, our very nature.

19.
Silence

Silence shared
Is such intimacy
And in the intricacy
Of that stillness we dared
Beyond some further threshold.
Faith and reason may contend
While mystery yet unfolds
Where they can neither apprehend.

Silence is a better prayer,
A more fitting experiment,
If we would but defer
Such bitter argument.
There are no final solutions;
Love alone is absolution.

20.
Become

The weight of weightlessness,
A wafer on the tongue
So subtle to taste—
Like death — and then it's gone.
Abundance in emptiness,
Unapparent at first,
We make its promise
Unquenchable thirst.

The nails go in
The cross goes up
The shattering pain
The loss of hope.
The suffocating death—
Then — become another breath.

21.
Love

Is it in the leaves?
The die cast? The milk spilt?
Whatever we might believe
Irrelevant?
This tiny blue fleck
Caught in brief sunlight,
Floating in its amniotic sac
Of atmosphere whose hand we bite
That's fed us well this far.
Where do we go from here?
I've loved you from the start,
And still do, I fear!
What redemption might we find,
We who have been too long blind?

22.
Homeless – September 2020

(with thanks to Jason Isbell)

We met in outer space,
Two alien souls,
And died in inner space
To become one whole.
We formed a quantum quest—
Being light years apart
From those who are closest—
The entanglement of hearts.
Perhaps we never loved,
But rather love loved us
And we simply dissolved
In its stream of loss.
Now love is a pipe bomb ready to
blow
And we are homeless with nothing
to show.

23.
Neighbours

I am a sandcastle
As the tide swells,
An empty vessel
Where love dwells.
I am just a bubble,
A sphere of light and moisture—
Emptiness ineffable—
I am love's cloister.

It's hard to live a good life
In a world so hateful
Where belief fights belief
And greed tramples the grateful
And indifference yet unmoved?
All we do is love and be loved.

24.
Apostasy

Consumerism is a cult
And cults are hard to leave;
It causes much tumult
When you no longer believe.
You hear the wilderness calling,
Leave family and friends behind.
Your actions seem appalling
To the devotionally blind.

Earth burns, her children pay the
price.
Celebrity and GDP,
Those insatiable deities,
Demand endless sacrifice.
In the wilderness your lone voice—
Community begins with choice.

25.
Mystery

I have only this body,
This sinking vessel,
That tides and eddies
Will soon undwell.

Then, only mind—
Thoughts arise and leave,
Entangle and unwind—
An empty sieve.

Then, only emptiness,
Or rather it has me
And I am undressed
Till even that i is ceased
Beyond existence—
Then — only Mystery—

26.
The Weather

The future is dark
Probably for the best
Not knowing its arc
We have to dig deepest
To pull together
Look out for one another
Every sister and brother
Because the weather
Is only getting worse—
That's down to us
That's the curse
The terrible injustice
We bequeath to coming
generations.
Time to be united more than
nations.

27.
Unsettled

*(imo those who died,
Carrickmines 10th October 2015)*

I've never been to a halting site,
Those places always scare me.
I know that's not right
But "those people" dare me
To look at myself
In the mirror of my soul
And see I need *your* help
If we're to be whole.
Jesus was a mincéir
From the outskirts of town,
And we so blind to dare
That he should settle down.
Jesus is the migrant who makes
us see
We have to be unsettled to be free.

28.
Stuck in Neutral

We're neutral, you see,
We don't see the flights
That come and go in the night
From the land of the free.
We hold the middle ground
And follow the third way
Of looking the other way,
Our heads firmly in the sand.
We appreciate the price—
The children's selfless giving
For our standard of living—
Their heroic sacrifice.
That's the murderous banality
Of our pious neutrality.

29.
Broken

These imaginal cells
Silent sonatas of light
Whose secrets I spell
In the dark of night.

These broken sonnets
Emerge from the hidden
Wanted or not
Arise unbidden.

These bright scattered stones
Catching moonlight
Illuminate the dark zones
That mark my flight—
My unbroken fall
Through depthless soul.

30.
Adrift

Give god a laugh, show ‘em your
plans.
Win or lose, there’s no success,
That’s not the appropriate lens;
Forget about progress.
Adrift on the sea of Tao
Leave your compass behind;
Through the darkness from your bow
Your charts and sextant are blind.
This craft is headed for the rocks,
You have no need of siren song
To guide you, so don’t be shocked—
That’s been your course all along.
Now, as the waves begin to spill
And your little boat dips her sail…

31.
Starlings

Each of us a coalescence
Of disparate elements
Configured to an essence
Derived from flow and sequence
Whose meaning may at a glance
Shift and change to something new—
Murmurations of circumstance
Our certainties all undo.

Our suchness is in flow,
We are conductors of light.
Our gift is letting go,
Always unrequited
To any perfect existence—
Lives spent unlearning resistance.

32.
Re-member

(with thanks to Pema Chödrön)

Lives of mistaken identity,
Of glimpses caught in passing
windows;
Hearts made to be free,
Grown blind to wondrous views.
We've forgotten we're indigenous,
That we belong to the land
And so have lost our place
In these unravelling strands.

Remember who we are—
First, do no harm
For we are warriors;
We take care of one another
And embrace the world as it is.
Remember, we belong to this.

33.
Walking

(for Naoimh & Fiona)

Saturday mornings were the best,
The three of us together,
And later a silent guest;
We would walk forever.
Some souls walk through desert,
Through famine and through fire,
Walking with all they're worth—
Just the clothes they wear.
How can I walk away?
These worlds live inside me
Formed from the same clay,
Wherever I go they find me:
Dead man walking down a lonely
road,
A dead tree fallen in the singing
woods.

34.
Supernova

I carry this resentment,
A log for both my eyes,
While feigning contentment.
So why am I surprised
When everything falls apart?
What did I expect?
Do I think the heart
Is something to protect?

When a heart implodes
A black hole forms
Or else it explodes
With spectacular light storms.
Undertaker-midwife—
Death delivers life.

35.
Cells

Trees perform wonderful tonglen,
Each leaf's cells' photosynthesis
Absorbing carbon and toxins
While emitting loving kindness.
Something we could emulate
To interrupt the path
That winds from fear to hate
Through the raging forest fires of
wrath
That have engulfed our soul.
Or is it too late?
Too far beyond control
To have already sealed our fate?
Hope is the action we can choose;
It only fails if we refuse.

36.
Evensong

Let the blackbird sing;
What better blessing
To celebrate the evening—
My prayer is listening.
Let the sunset stream in
Through the filtering trees
Played by a gentle breeze—
My song is seeing.
If I close my eyes
The sky is just as blue.
Later on the moon will rise—
Clouded or clear, her gaze is true.
There's nothing done that need be
unlived—
Life is not something to be solved.

37.
Small

When you look in the mirror
And no one is there
It can cause a stir
But answers the prayer:
How to live authentic
In a world so real,
When action feels fake
But silence is cruel.

I met the Buddha on the road
And before I killed him he said:
We have to become really small
To make it through the needle's eye
And life is just another wall,
We spend it learning to die.

38.
H_2O

Again, washed up on the shores of lost
And if not lost, then deluded.
Being found, there is no cost,
Just everything included.
We live these iceberg lives
Mostly below the surface
Holding our breath till truth arrives—
This melting life so nervous.

You know, water is our true state,
So how could we ever drown?
We're more likely to evaporate
And even then to come back down.
So, you may persist to struggle in
vain,
To resist the consolations of rain.

39.
Be

My body the earth,
The earth my soul;
Ever before my birth
I am whole.
I am the soil,
I am harvest and death;
I am every child
That ever draws breath.
The river my song,
The hills my history,
Each day that dawns—
The pulse of mystery.
So many ways to *be*,
To shed not being free.

40.
After the Tannery

(for the Chestnutters)

We had churches for prayer
And schools for learning,
A cinema and town square;
The graveyard for mourning.
We swam in the Barrow
And walked in Corrig wood
We were Winesburg, Ohio,
Every small town neighbourhood.
We milled our flour,
Harvested the turf.
But then there came an hour
When no one cried, *Enough!*
And so, everything soured
As the phantom feline purred.

41.
Avatar

Ego is the avatar
For this no-self existence,
You can drive it like a car
And it will go the distance.
Direction is another matter,
For that you need a soul
Pointing towards the mystery star—
And so the road unfolds.

You are not your name,
You have no reputation,
No use for shame,
No cause for celebration.
Only mystery is true;
Remember, you are — not you.

42.
Moonlight

Heart and Mind sat down with
Source
To hold a conversation,
The subject of their discourse—
To conduct an investigation
Into the nature of being.
Mind argued rationally
While Heart pleaded passionately
With Source quietly listening.
Then, as the conversation slowed
And everyone grew quiet,
Out of the shadowed
Body, as soft as moonlight,
It was Silence herself who spoke
In words none alone could invoke.

43.
Many Rooms

(imo Alan Kurdi, died 2nd September 2015)

In my father's house…
The mysteries of the multiverse
Hidden within us—
Here lies the source.

Its currency is kindness,
An end to all our killing,
To cure our pact with blindness—
We are kin to all that's living.

Its language is silence,
Our tears its rivers
And on the shores of abundance
Are we delivered
Each to each other,
Migrants all, — together…

44.
Contrary

(for the victims & survivors)

My namesake and saint,
Fallen – so-called, ill-accused,
Named for another, it's you I choose
Despite my former complaint.
You, who followed love
When others wanted power—
And so, misread the hour—
Only you had the resolve
To be faithful to the end
And all the new beginnings
To which those in need of winning
Are always blind.
You were contrary in that way.
We're still blind today.

45.
Intimacy

(for Thomas Berry)

The same river twice?
Not possible, they say;
It's not just your choice,
The river has its way.

The gardener tends the soil—
Weed, hoe, feed, sow—
For all that careful toil
Earth and element make it grow.

And so, you take your seat
To sit and contemplate,
But it's the energies
Of countless galaxies
With which we participate—
Kosmos and sitter — one intimacy.

46.
Fireflies

We set these little boats aflame
And launch them into the darkness
Not knowing what becomes of them
Before they slip beneath the surface.
Their voyages are their own,
Their fates not our concern;
They sail for shores unknown
Lighting the darkness as they burn.
We must not ask too much
Nor try to stake some claim;
Who knows what lives they touch,
What hearts they set aflame?
And so, like fireflies in the night,
Let's set this darkness burning bright.